The Skydiving Beavers
A True Tale

Written by *Susan Wood* and Illustrated by *Gÿsbert van Frankenhuyzen*

It all started when the folks of McCall, Idaho, realized they had a problem.

A big problem.

A big, beaver-type problem.

McCall, in Idaho's woodsy backcountry, was a lovely place. Trees so tall, they touched the sky. Crisp mountain air. And, oh, that sparkling blue lake.

Swimming and hiking in the summer, skiing and snowmen in the winter. Who wouldn't want to live there? People rushed to build homes and lodges on the shore, docks for their sailboats and canoes, and paved roads to get to it all.

Trouble was, that lakeside land had already been claimed.
For decades—centuries, even—beavers had been the only
ones doing the building there.

Beavers feel right at home on land and in water. For protection
from critters that think they'd make a tasty snack, beavers build
dams, then hide in the deep water behind the dam. Beavers
build their dams with wood they harvest by gnawing down
trees—lots and lots of trees.

Now the beavers had a problem too.

A big problem.

A big, people-type problem.

Where the beavers once built their dams, now there were boaters and swimmers. Where the beavers once gathered wood for dams and food, now there were houses and people.

And where the people tried to drive their cars, now water flooded the roads because of the dams. Where the people wanted to enjoy their backyard views, now trees toppled left and right, thanks to all the gnawing.

The people were muscling in on the beavers' habitat. And the beavers were trashing the people's habitat. A real turf war. It seemed McCall just wasn't big enough for everybody.

So, what to do?

One man named Elmo Heter had an idea. Elmo had a lot of experience with beavers, working as he did for the Idaho Department of Fish and Game. He knew just what beavers needed to live happily and peacefully: wide-open spaces with plenty of trees, loads of rivers and creeks—and absolutely no people around.

Elmo knew of a place just like that: the Chamberlain Basin, many miles away. Acre after acre of deep, dense forest. Fresh mountain streams and ponds. Pure wilderness, untouched by humans—a neighborhood where the beavers would feel right at home.

But Elmo had a problem.

A big problem.

A big, transportation-type problem.

How do you move a bunch of beavers to a place with no roads, no railway, no airport, and no bus station?

Elmo thought about using horses or mules. He could round up the beavers, put them in cages, load them on the pack animals, and hoof it a few days into the wilderness. But Elmo knew that long, rough trips would make beavers mighty grumpy, and that horses and mules would get spooked and ornery when loaded with unhappy beavers. No—beavers, horses, and mules just don't mix.

Then Elmo remembered the piles of parachutes left over from World War II, which had ended just a few years before. What if he dropped the beavers from a plane?

Skydiving beavers?

Well, why not?

Elmo had his plan.

Now he needed to figure
out how to make it work.

One of Elmo's early ideas was to put the beavers in a box made of woven willow branches. He thought that once the box parachuted to the ground, the beavers inside would gnaw their way to freedom.

After more pondering, though, Elmo tossed that idea.

Beavers were grade-A, gold-star chewers. The beavers might chew their way out too soon. They might run loose in the plane. Or they might pop out mid-skydive!

Elmo came up with another idea.

How about a box that opened automatically when it landed?

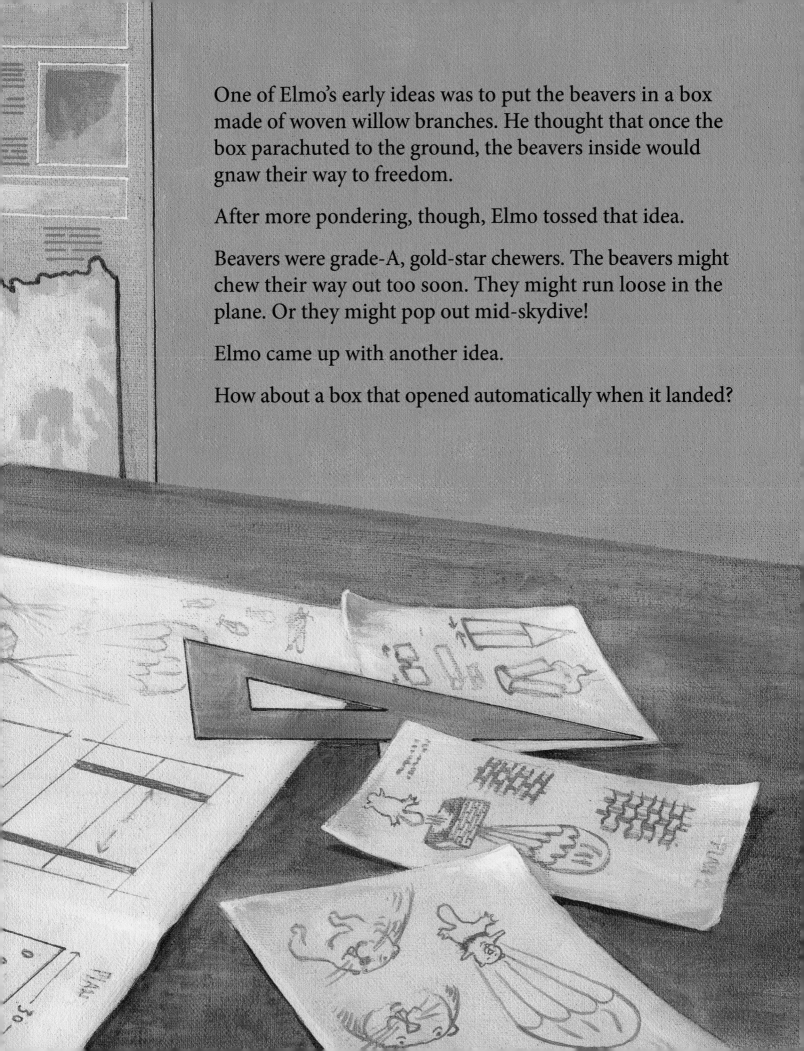

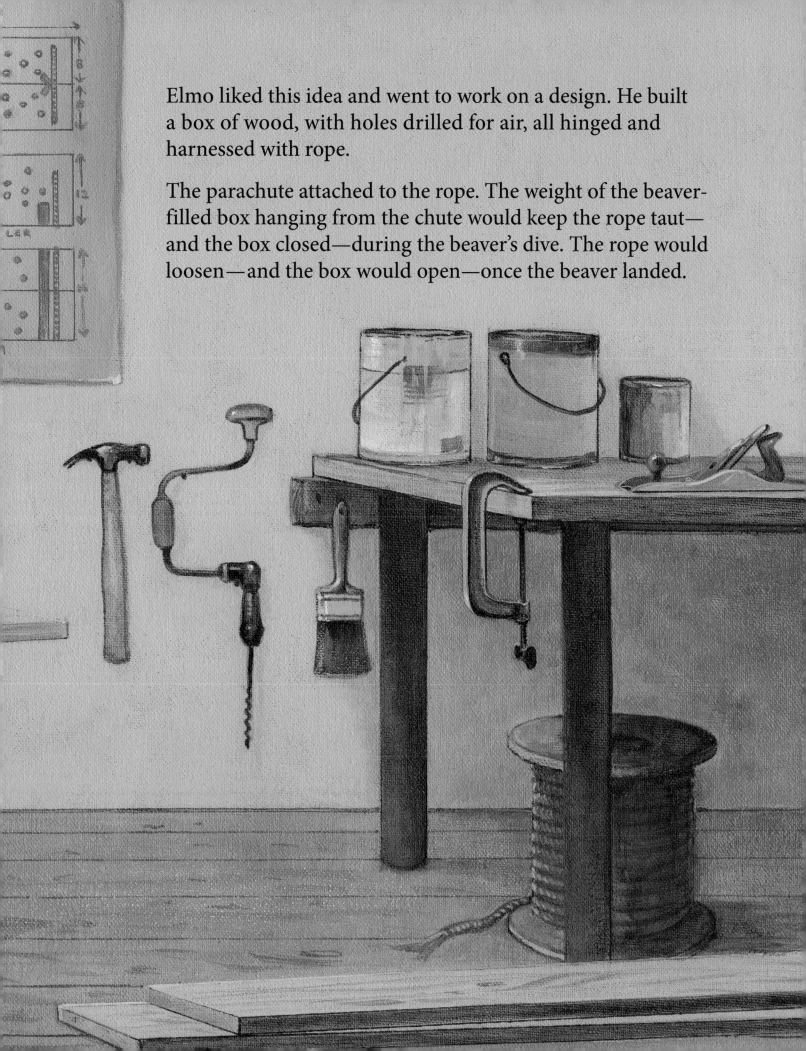

Elmo liked this idea and went to work on a design. He built a box of wood, with holes drilled for air, all hinged and harnessed with rope.

The parachute attached to the rope. The weight of the beaver-filled box hanging from the chute would keep the rope taut—and the box closed—during the beaver's dive. The rope would loosen—and the box would open—once the beaver landed.

Elmo needed to test his nifty self-opening beaver-drop box.
He put together a team and did a few experiments with weights.
The box opened every time.

Now he needed the real thing—a beaver. Elmo corralled an
old male beaver into the box. He named the beaver Geronimo.

Elmo fastened a parachute to the box. A pilot took the box up in a plane. When the plane buzzed low over Elmo's test field, the box was dropped.

The chute bloomed like a buttercup, then caught the breeze. Elmo surely held his breath. The box fell as gently as a mountain snowflake, landing softly on the grass. The box sprang open . . . and Geronimo scrambled out!

The parachute plan worked!

But Elmo needed to be sure that the parachute plan would work *every* time—not just this once. So he and his team tested again …

　　　… and again …

　　　　　… and again …

After a while, it seemed Geronimo was growing to like all the skydiving. Each time he touched down and the box sprang open, he'd scurry out … then crawl right back in for another go.

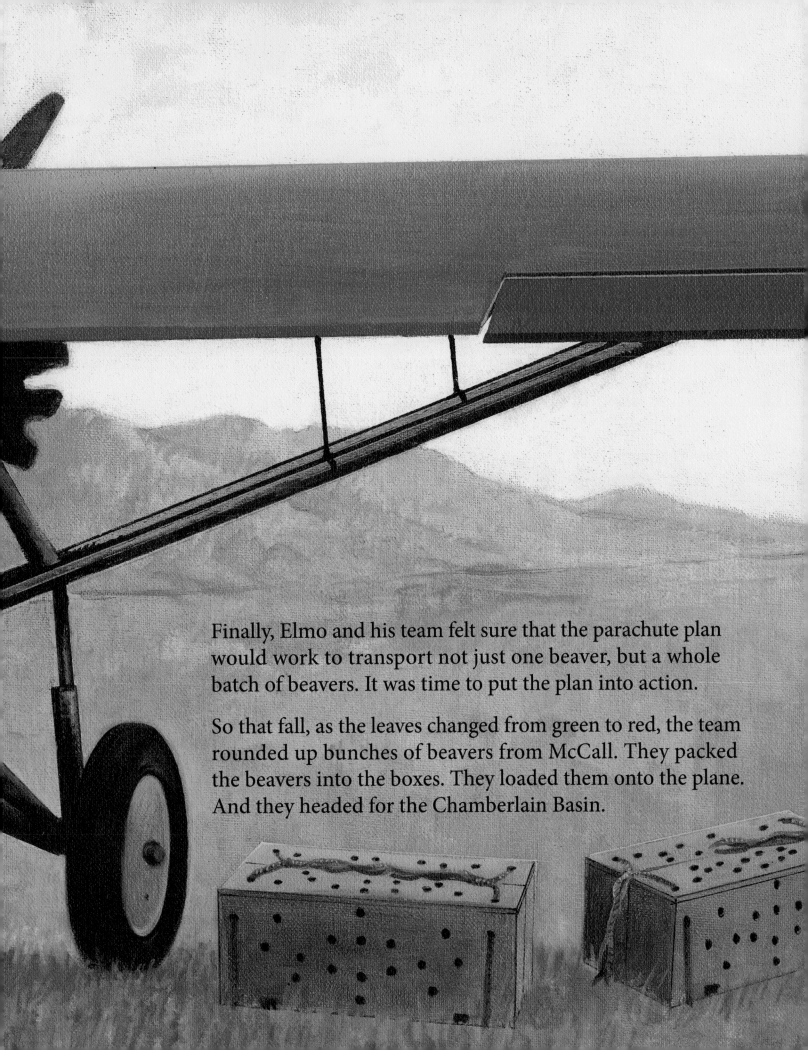

Finally, Elmo and his team felt sure that the parachute plan would work to transport not just one beaver, but a whole batch of beavers. It was time to put the plan into action.

So that fall, as the leaves changed from green to red, the team rounded up bunches of beavers from McCall. They packed the beavers into the boxes. They loaded them onto the plane. And they headed for the Chamberlain Basin.

The pilot buzzed low over the thick forests, looking for the grassy meadow the team had selected for the drop. There it was! The team readied the chutes.

Three . . .

Two . . .

One . . .

Now!

The chutes whooshed open . . .

. . . and beavers fell from the sky.

They wafted like falling leaves on the autumn wind to their new woodsy patch of paradise.

And the first to hit the ground? Geronimo!

With his nose leading him to water, there he and the other beavers could build a happy, peaceful home.

Author's Note

As unbelievable as it sounds, beavers really did fall from the sky over backwoods Idaho. In 1948, Elmo Heter and his team from the Idaho Department of Fish and Game air-dropped seventy-six live beavers into the Chamberlain Basin region, in what is now part of the Frank Church–River of No Return Wilderness.

Geronimo was the very first to be transported, along with three young female beavers. He and the females landed safely, though Geronimo took his time leaving his opened box. Perhaps he was waiting for another dive!

Seventy-five of the seventy-six skydiving beavers landed without problems, and were surely delighted with their new people-free habitat. On one of the boxes, though, a rope lashing loosened some distance above the ground. The curious beaver inside managed to climb out and onto the top of the box, jumping or falling before the box touched down.

Observations made a year later revealed that the beaver relocation was a total success. As Elmo reported in a 1950 issue of *The Journal of Wildlife Management*, the beavers had "built dams, constructed houses, stored up food, and were well on their way to producing colonies."

While Elmo's beaver relocation by parachute was an inventive idea in 1948, it likely wouldn't happen today. Scientists have since learned that beaver communities can be good for the environment, providing habitat and food sources for other wildlife and helping with water management. So these days, people find ways to get along with their neighborhood beavers. In Martinez, California, for example, a male and female beaver built an enormous dam across a local creek and chewed through willow trees and other city landscaping. When the city council wanted to exterminate the beavers because they feared the dammed creek would flood, Martinez residents organized to protect the animals.

The problem was solved by running a pipe through the beavers' dam to control water levels and flow. Thanks to the beavers, Alhambra Creek, once a fairly lifeless trickle, was transformed into a series of dams and ponds that are now home to a wider diversity of wildlife, including various fish, the North American river otter, and mink.

Though we may not transplant beavers anymore, it's still fun to think that the descendants of daredevil Geronimo and his fellow skydiving rodents are likely alive, well, and happily gnawing deep in the wilds of Idaho.

Bet you didn't know that beavers...

- Give off a goo that smells like vanilla—and you may have eaten it. Castoreum, a chemical compound sometimes used in vanilla flavoring, comes from a beaver's castor sacs, located under its tail. The brown stuff looks like molasses and smells like musky vanilla.

- Have orange front teeth. And it isn't because they forgot to brush. Those super-strong chompers that can gnaw through tree trunks are iron fortified. It's the iron in the tooth enamel that makes beavers' front teeth so strong, self-sharpening, and orange!

- Have multitasking tails. A beaver's flat, leathery tail serves many functions. In the water, the animal uses it like a boat rudder to maneuver around, or slaps it on the surface to warn other beavers of danger, such as an approaching predator. On land, the beaver's tail can work like a kickstand, helping the beaver sit upright, or as a counterbalance so the beaver won't tip over when carrying heavy tree limbs.

- Navigate in water with cool adaptations. Beavers have evolved built-in nose- and earplugs that keep out water, plus see-through "third eyelids," membranes that act as swim goggles covering their eyes. And their lips close *behind* their big front teeth, so they can carry food and building materials underwater without drowning.

- Were once ginormous! Beavers' Ice Age ancestors, called *Castoroides*, grew to seven feet long and nearly three hundred pounds. Now that's one big beaver!

Sources:

Heter, Elmo W. "Transplanting Beavers by Airplane and Parachute." *The Journal of Wildlife Management*. Vol. 14, No. 2 (April 1950), pp. 143–147.

Worth a Dam website, www.martinezbeavers.org.

Wright, Samantha. "Parachuting Beavers into Idaho's Wilderness? Yes, It Really Happened." Boise State Public Radio website, http://boisestatepublicradio.org/post/parachuting-beavers-idahos-wilderness-yes-it-really-happened. (January 14, 2015)

For Ava, who got me believing in skydiving beavers

Susan

ILLUSTRATOR'S ACKNOWLEDGMENTS
From the Idaho Department of Fish and Game: thanks to Sharon Clark, department historian
and archivist, for all your help in finding much-needed archival material; to Steve Nadeau,
wildlife biologist, and to Regan Berkley, wildlife manager, for pointing me in the right direction
(and all the back roads) during my research trip to Idaho.

Thanks to Becky Schwarz, Annie Fanta, and Geoff Gamble.
And a special big thanks and hugs to my grandkids, Noorah and Zayd, for being my kid models.

Gijsbert

Text Copyright © 2017 Susan Wood
Illustration Copyright © 2017 Gijsbert van Frankenhuyzen

Sleeping Bear Press®
2395 South Huron Parkway, Suite 200
Ann Arbor, MI 48104
www.sleepingbearpress.com

Printed and bound in the United States.

10 9 8 7 6 5 4

Library of Congress Cataloging-in-Publication Data

Names: Wood, Susan, 1965- author. | Frankenhuyzen, Gijsbert van, illustrator.
Title: The skydiving beavers : a true tale / written by Susan Wood ;
illustrated by Gijsbert van Frankenhuyzen.
Description: Ann Arbor, MI : Sleeping Bear Press, 2017.
Identifiers: LCCN 2016026769 | ISBN 9781585369942
Subjects: LCSH: Beavers—Idaho—Juvenile literature. | Wildlife
relocation—Idaho—Juvenile literature.
Classification: LCC QL737.R632 W66 2017 | DDC 599.3709796—dc23
LC record available at https://lccn.loc.gov/2016026769